SECOND EDITION

American Start with English

Student Book 3

D. H. Howe

OXFORD UNIVERSITY PRESS

Oxford University Press

198 Madison Avenue
New York, NY 10016 USA

Great Clarendon Street
Oxford OX2 6DP England

Oxford New York
Athens Auckland Bangkok Bogota Bombay
Buenos Aires Calcutta Cape Town Dar es Salaam Delhi
Florence Hong Kong Istanbul Karachi Kuala Lumpur
Madras Madrid Melbourne Mexico City Nairobi
Paris Singapore Taipei Tokyo Toronto Warsaw

and associated companies in
Berlin Ibadan

OXFORD is a trademark of Oxford University Press.

ISBN 0-19-434021-X

EDITORIAL MANAGER: Shelagh Speers
EDITOR: Edward Yoshioka
ASSISTANT EDITOR: Lynne Robertson
PRODUCTION AND DESIGN: OUP International Education Unit
and Oxprint Design
ASSOCIATE PRODUCTION EDITOR: Joseph McGasko
PRODUCTION COORDINATOR: Ahmad Sadiq
PRODUCTION MANAGER: Abram Hall

COVER DESIGN: April Okano
COVER PHOTOGRAPH: Alan Kaplan

ILLUSTRATIONS: Val Biro

Printing (last digit): 10 9 8 7 6 5 4 3

Printed in Hong Kong

Contents

Contents

Review

A: Look at Number 1. What is it?
B: It is an airplane.

1. airplane	2. cupboard	3. door	4. arm
5. shirt	6. eye	7. key	8. newspaper
9. pocket	10. baby	11. shop	12. window
13. picture	14. wheel	15. finger	16. ear
17. check	18. foot	19. doll	20. mouth

Review

1. house	2. teacher	3. leg	4. teacher
5. bus driver	6. bicycle	7. police officer	8. cow
9. boy	10. cake	11. nose	12. girl
13. man	14. fly	15. mail carrier	16. woman
17. street	18. face	19. handkerchief	20. hand
21. room	22. star	23. cookie	24. knee

1. A: Look at Number 1. Is it a pencil?
   B: No, it is not. It is not a pencil.
   A: Is it a house?
   B: Yes, it is. It is a house.

2. A: Look at Number 2. Is she a police officer?
   B: No, she is not. She is not a police officer.
   A: Is she a teacher?
   B: Yes, she is. She is a teacher.

Read and practice.

A: What is your name?
B: My name is Mary.
A: Are you a girl?
B: Yes, I am. I am a girl.
A: Are you a boy?
B: No, I am not. I am not a boy.
A: What is your father's name?
B: His name is Mr. Bell.
A: Is that your book?
B: Yes, this is my book.

Review

1. car
2. boat
3. bowl
4. bus
5. lamp
6. cake
7. telephone
8. spoon
9. umbrella
10. flower
11. ball
12. banana

1. A: Look at Number 1. What is this?
   B: It is a car.
   A: What color is it?
   B: It is blue. It is a blue car.
   A: Where is the blue car?
   B: It is under the green table.

2. A: Look at Number 1. Is there a car under the table?
   B: Yes, there is. There is a car under the table.

Review

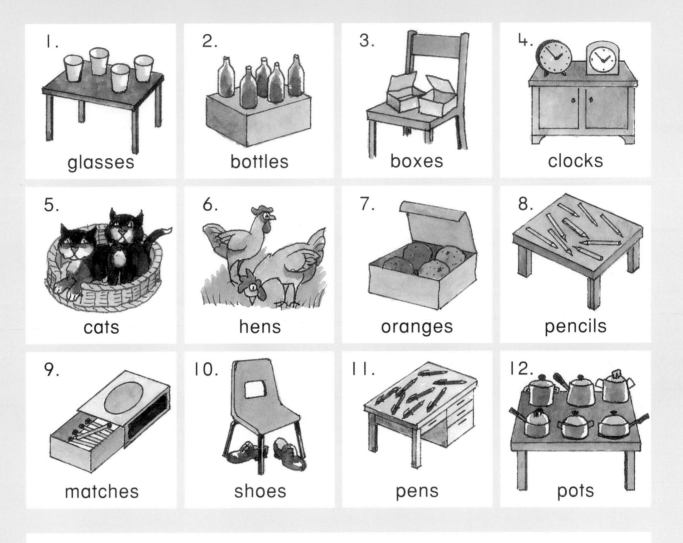

1. glasses
2. bottles
3. boxes
4. clocks
5. cats
6. hens
7. oranges
8. pencils
9. matches
10. shoes
11. pens
12. pots

1. A: Look at Number 1. What are these?
   B: They are glasses.
   A: What color are they?
   B: They are green. They are green glasses.
   A: Where are the green glasses?
   B: They are on the brown table.

2. A: Look at Number 1.
      How many glasses are there on the table?
   B: There are four glasses on the table.

Review

1. running
2. walking
3. standing
4. sitting
5. smiling
6. crying
7. eating
8. drinking
9. jumping
10. falling
11. pushing
12. pulling

1. A: Look at Number 1. Is he walking?
   B: No, he is not. He is not walking.
   A: What is he doing?
   B: He is running.

2. A: Look at Number 3. Are they sitting?
   B: No, they are not. They are not sitting.
   A: What are they doing?
   B: They are standing.

1. holding
2. walking
3. waiting
4. carrying
5. climbing
6. standing
7. drawing
8. riding

1. A: Look at Number 1. What is she doing?
   B: She is holding a book.

2. A: Look at Number 2. What is he doing?
   B: He is walking to the door.

3. A: Look at Number 3. What is she doing?
   B: She is waiting for a bus at a bus stop.

Read and practice.

A: What are you doing?
B: I am holding my pencil.

1. John

2. Mary and Mimi

3. Peter

4. John and Mary

5. Miss Lee

6. Mr. Bell

7. Ann

8. Ann and Mary

9. Mimi

10. All the girls

11. Mr. Green

12. Tom

13. A dog

14. Peter

15. All the boys

16. All the boys   All the girls

1. A: Who has a red shirt?
   B: John does. He has a red shirt.

2. A: Who has a blue dress?
   B: Mary and Mimi do. They have blue dresses.

3. A: Who is kicking the ball?
   B: Peter is. He is kicking the ball.

Read and practice.

A:

Please	open close point at touch shut	the door. the window. your desk. your book. your eyes.

B:

I am	opening closing pointing at touching shutting	the door. the window. my desk. my book. my eyes.

Review

Read the questions. Then say the answers.

 1. What is your name?
 2. Are you a boy?
 3. Are you a girl?
 4. What is your teacher's name?
 5. How old are you?
 6. What are you doing now?
 7. What is there on your desk?
 8. What are you holding in your hand?
 9. What is your teacher holding in her hand?
10. What color is your book?
11. What are your friends doing?
12. What is your teacher doing?
13. How many boys are there in the room?
14. How many girls are there in the room?
15. Where is the blackboard?

Read and practice.

What color is	sugar? grass? salt? milk? ink?	Sugar Grass Salt Milk Ink	is	green. white. blue.

Uncountable nouns

1.

   This is a piece of chalk.

2.

   This is a piece of wood.

3.

   This is a piece of cake.

4.

   This is a piece of string.

5.

   This is a piece of paper.

6.

   This is a glass of water.

7.

   This is a bottle of milk.

8.

   This is a bowl of soup.

9.

   This is a bottle of ink.

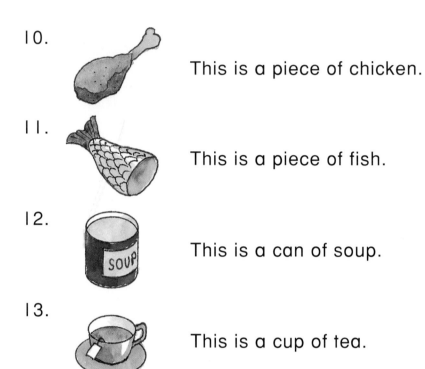

10. This is a piece of chicken.

11. This is a piece of fish.

12. This is a can of soup.

13. This is a cup of tea.

Practice questions and answers like these.

A: Look at Number 1. What is it?

B: It is a glass of milk.

A: Look at Number 2. What is it?

B: It is a piece of string.

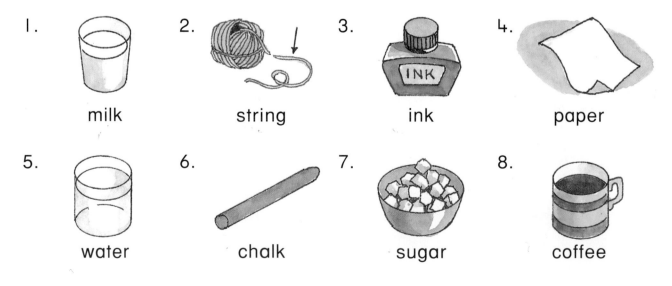

1. milk

2. string

3. ink

4. paper

5. water

6. chalk

7. sugar

8. coffee

1.

Can she sing?
Yes, she can.

2.

Can he sing?
No, he cannot.

3.

Can she hear?
No, she cannot.

4.

Can he hear?
Yes, he can.

5.

Can he see?
No, he cannot.

6.

Can he see?
Yes, he can.

7.

Can she speak?
No, she cannot.

8. Can Mary swim?
Yes, she can.

9. Can Mimi cook?
No, she cannot.

10. Can Mr. Lowe drive a bus?
Yes, he can.

11. Can John ride a bicycle?
No, he cannot.

12. Can the men carry the box?
Yes, they can.

13. Can you see the bird in the tree?
Yes, I can.

14. Can you see the man in the sea?
Yes, I can.

1.

I like apples.

2.

I like oranges.

3.

I like bananas.

4.

I like candy.

5. They like cake.

6. They like ice cream.

1.

He likes the dog.

2.

She likes the cat.

3.

She likes the yellow flower.

4. I like the red clock.

Thank you.

He likes the red clock.

Review

A. Make six good sentences.

Please give me a	piece glass bottle bowl piece cup	of	water. chicken. soup. ink. tea. paper.

B. Answer the questions.
1. Can a fish swim?
2. Can a cow fly?
3. Can a dog swim?
4. Can a cat swim?
5. Can you swim?

C. Make five sentences beginning: I like ...

D. Make three sentences beginning: My friend likes ...

1.

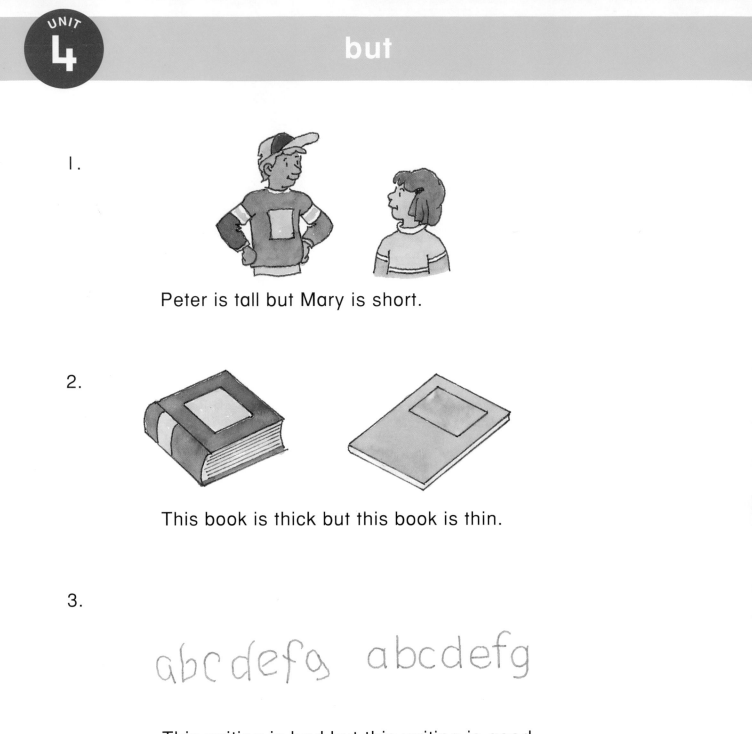

Peter is tall but Mary is short.

2.

This book is thick but this book is thin.

3.

This writing is bad but this writing is good.

4.

This board is white but this marker is green.

1.

Mary can swim but she cannot ride a bicycle.

2.

Mimi can sing but she cannot cook.

3.

The men can carry the box but they cannot carry the tree.

4.

Mr. Lowe can drive a bus but he cannot fly an airplane.

Read.

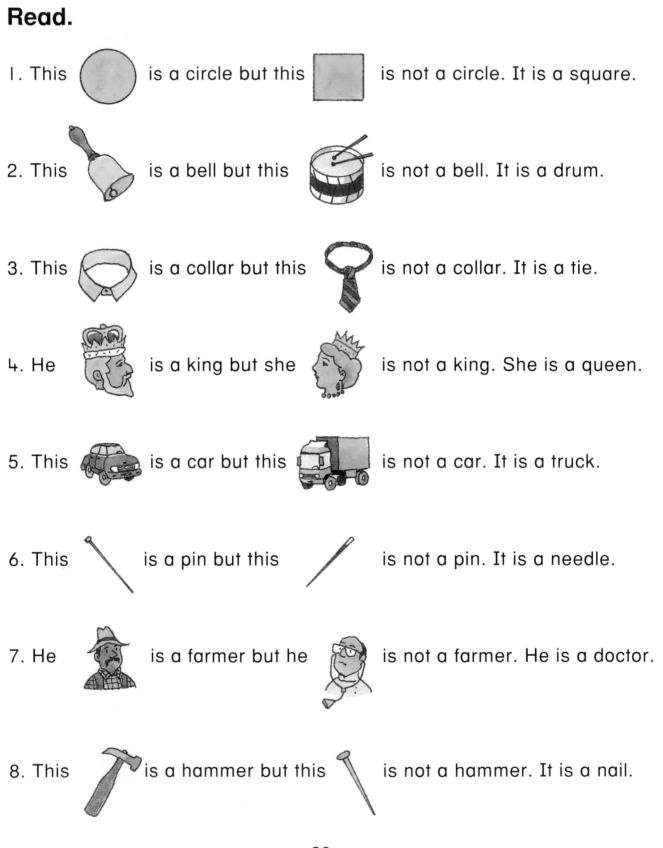

1. This ⬤ is a circle but this ◼ is not a circle. It is a square.

2. This 🔔 is a bell but this 🥁 is not a bell. It is a drum.

3. This 👔 is a collar but this 👔 is not a collar. It is a tie.

4. He 👑 is a king but she 👸 is not a king. She is a queen.

5. This 🚗 is a car but this 🚚 is not a car. It is a truck.

6. This is a pin but this is not a pin. It is a needle.

7. He 🧑‍🌾 is a farmer but he 🧑‍⚕️ is not a farmer. He is a doctor.

8. This 🔨 is a hammer but this is not a hammer. It is a nail.

Read aloud.

a	apple	bag	black	cat	fan
e	bed	bell	desk	egg	hen
i	finger	fish	lips	milk	pin
o	bottle	box	clock	dog	dots
u	bus	button	cup	duck	numbers

A rhyme to learn.

Ice cream is cold but fire is hot.

A circle is round but a square is not.

A kitten is weak but a horse is strong.

Monday   A day is short but a year is long.

1996

21

1.

This is a pen and that is a pencil.

2.

This is a bag and that is a box.

3.

This is a book and that is a picture.

4.

This is a flower and that is a tree.

5.

This is a bird and that is an airplane.

1.

These are glasses and those are bottles.

2.

These are apples and those are oranges.

3.

These are shoes and those are socks.

4.

These are cats and those are dogs.

5.

These are girls and those are boys.

1.

This window is open but that window is shut.

2.

This bag is small but that bag is big.

3.

This car is old but that car is new.

4.

These apples are red but those apples are green.

5.

These bottles are empty but those bottles are full.

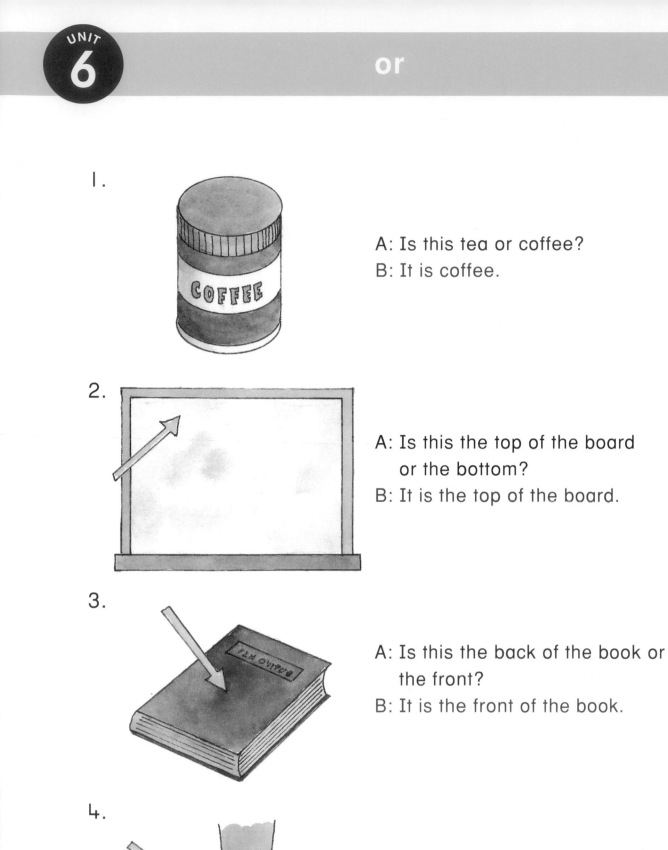

1.

A: Is this tea or coffee?
B: It is coffee.

2.

A: Is this the top of the board or the bottom?
B: It is the top of the board.

3.

A: Is this the back of the book or the front?
B: It is the front of the book.

4.

A: Is this an ankle or a knee?
B: It is an ankle.

Read and answer the questions.

1. Is that a bird or an airplane?

   It is an airplane.

2. Is that the sun or a star?

3. Are those cars or trucks?

4. Are those pens or pencils?

5. Are those hats or coats?

1.  Is this glass full or empty?

2. $\begin{array}{r} 298.765 \\ +\ 89.474 \\ \hline \end{array}$ Is this easy or hard?

3. Is this shirt wet or dry?

Read aloud.

a	hand	man	matches	pan	hat
e	leg	neck	pen	pencil	red
i	pin	ship	stick	picture	window
o	pot	socks	orange	collar	doll
u	cup	truck	sun	thumb	umbrella

A. Answer the questions.

    1. Is ice cold or hot?

    2. Is water wet or dry?

    3. Is a horse strong or weak?

    4. Is walking easy or hard?

    5. Is a pin small or big?

    6. Is a page of a book thin or thick?

B. Put in is or are.

    1. Ice is cold but fire _____ hot.

    2. Trees are big but matches _____ small.

    3. Horses _____ strong but kittens _____ weak.

    4. We _____ boys but they _____ girls.

    5. Collars _____ round but ties _____ not.

    6. _____ a blackboard white or black?

    7. _____ milk black or white?

    8. _____ matches big or small?

    9. _____ a year short or long?

  10. _____ apples red or blue?

C. Answer the questions.

    1. Are you writing with a pen or a pencil?

    2. Is this the top of the page or the bottom?

1.

Don't run.

Walk.

2.

Don't sit on the desk.

Sit on the chair.

3.

Don't write on the wall.

Write in your book.

4.

Don't look out the window.

Look at the board.

Don't

1.

Please don't walk on the grass.

Walk on the path.

2.

Please don't walk in the street.

Walk on the sidewalk.

3.

Please don't run across the street.

That is dangerous.

4.

Please don't fight.

That is naughty.

1. Please be quiet.

   Don't make a sound.

2. Please be careful.

   Don't break the glasses.

3. Please be careful.

   Don't be careless.

4. Please be quick.

   Don't be late for school.

Don't

A rhyme to learn. Don't run across the street.

Stop and look.

Don't write on the wall.

Write in your book.

Don't run in school.

Always walk.

Listen to the teacher.

Please don't talk.

Read aloud. Make the sounds long.

a	page	cake	face	plate	date
i	fire	nine	line	smile	knife

o stone those nose close home

u ruler use June

e these

1.

I am touching you.

You are touching me.

2.

I am touching Mary.

I am touching her.

I am touching John.

I am touching him.

3.

I am carrying a kitten.

I am carrying it.

1.

Listen to me, children.

I am teaching you.

Yes, you are teaching us.

2.

I am teaching the children.

I am teaching them.

How many sentences can you make?

He		touching	me.
	is	pointing at	him.
She		carrying	her.
		holding	it.
You		talking to	us.
	are	listening to	them.
They			

Read and answer the questions.

1. Is Mary helping her mother?

   Yes, she is. She is helping her.

2. Is John kicking the ball?

3. Is John catching the ball?

4. Is the dog playing with the children?

5. Are the children eating the oranges?

Read aloud.

ea = ee

| ear | sea | teacher | tea |

| eat | read | easy | hear |

| near | speak | please | clean |

| But: | head | bread | breakfast | pear |

Review

1. This is John. I am touching (him, her, it).

2. Miss Lee is talking. The children are listening to (him, her, it).

3. Don't open the door. Close (him, her, it).

4. The boys are listening. She is talking to (they, them, him).

5. We are listening to the teacher. She is talking to (we, her, us).

6. I am talking to the kitten. It is listening to (me, it, us).

1.

This is a bucket.

This is a bucket, too.

2.

This is a bowl.

This is a bowl, too.

3.

This is a package.

This is a package, too.

4.

This is a whistle.

This is a whistle, too.

5.

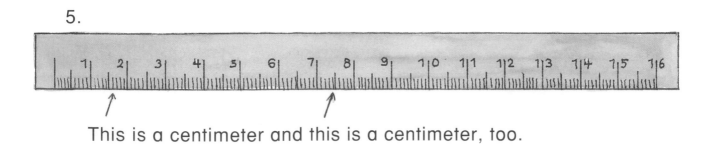

This is a centimeter and this is a centimeter, too.

1.  John is painting and

   Peter is painting, too.

2.  Mary is dancing and

   Ann is dancing, too.

3.  The boy is kneeling and

   the girl is kneeling, too.

4.  Mary is sewing and

   Ann is sewing, too.

5.  The cat is asleep and

   the baby is asleep, too.

Peter   Mary   John   Ann

Finish the sentences.

1. Peter's shirt is blue and John's shirt is blue, too.
2. Mary's dress is yellow and Ann's dress is ...
3. Peter's book is red and ...
4. Mary's basket ...
5. Peter's shoes are ...
6. Mary's shoes ...

Read aloud.

oo (long)	moon	room	root	spoon	school

too   tooth

oo (short)   book   cook   foot   cookie

look   good   wood

1. She has a pen and I have one, too.

2. He has a book and I have one, too.

3. She is wearing a skirt and I am wearing one, too.

4. This letter has a stamp and this letter has one, too.

5. This house has a gate and this house has one, too.

These are ships.

This ship has a flag.

This ship has a flag, too.
It is the same one.

This ship has a flag, too.
It is a different one.

Read aloud.

C = S

face	pencil	ceiling	centimeter
circle	ice	dance	ice cream

Peter   Mary   John   Ann

A. Read.

1. Peter has a kite and John has one, too.
2. Mary has a kitten and Ann has one, too.
3. Peter's shirt is blue and John's shirt is blue, too.
4. Mary's skirt is red and Ann's skirt is red, too.
5. Peter's socks are red and John's socks are red, too.
6. Mary's socks are green and Ann's socks are green, too.

B. Now make up sentences about May and Mimi.

May   Mimi

1.

The cat is little.
It is a little cat.
It is not a big cat.

2.

The woman is old.
She is an old woman.
She is not a young woman.

3.

The dog is long.
It is a long dog.
It is not a short dog.

4.

The boy is thin.
He is a thin boy.
He is not a fat boy.

5.

The cat is dirty.
It is a dirty cat.
It is not a clean cat.

6.

The man is unhappy.
He is an unhappy man.
He is not a happy man.

Adjectives

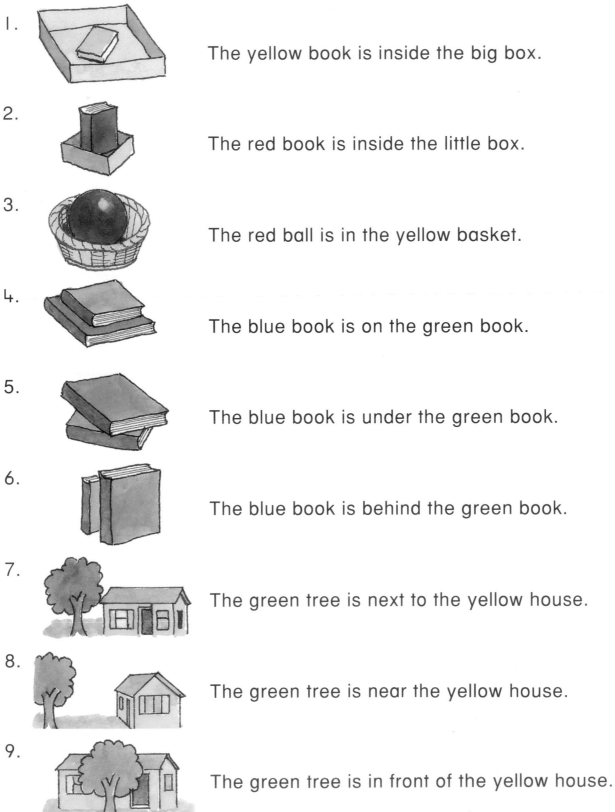

1. The yellow book is inside the big box.

2. The red book is inside the little box.

3. The red ball is in the yellow basket.

4. The blue book is on the green book.

5. The blue book is under the green book.

6. The blue book is behind the green book.

7. The green tree is next to the yellow house.

8. The green tree is near the yellow house.

9. The green tree is in front of the yellow house.

45

Adjectives

Read and answer the questions.

1. Is this a red flower or a yellow one?
It is a red one.

2. Is this a dirty shirt or a clean one?

3. Is he an old man or a young one?

4. Is this a big box or a small one?

5. Is this an old car or a new one?

6. Is this a white cat or a black one?

7. Is he a tall boy or a short one?

8. Is she a happy girl or an unhappy one?

9. Is this a small dog or a big one?

1.

Boys, hold up your books.

We are holding up our books.

Look at the boys.
They are holding up their books.

2.

Girls, hold up your rulers.

We are holding up our rulers.

Look at the girls.
They are holding up their rulers.

Read and answer the questions.

1. Look at the children.
   Where are their books?
   They are on their desks.
   Where are your books?
   Our books are on our desks.

2. Where are their rulers?
   Where are your rulers?

3. Where are their pens?
   Where are your pens?

4. What color is their classroom door?
   It is red.
   What color is your classroom door?

5. Look at the picture. Look at the dog.
   What color is its head?

6. Look at the picture. Look at the cat.
   What color is its tail?

Look at the dog.
Point to its tail.
Point to its head.
Point to its eyes.

Look at the cat.
Point to its tail.
Point to its head.
Point to its eyes.

Look at the cat and the dog.
Point to their tails.
Point to their heads.
Point to their eyes.

Read aloud.

ar

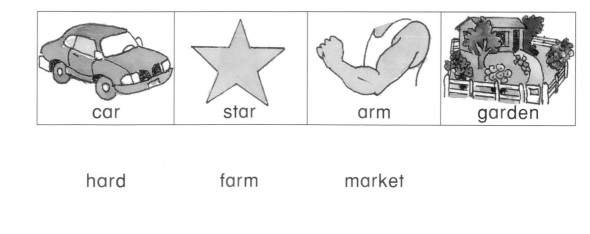

| car | star | arm | garden |

hard　　　　farm　　　　market

But:　　　carry

1.

Look at the doll.

Does it have any legs?

Does it have any arms?

It has some legs but it doesn't have any arms.

2.

Look at the man.

Does he have any boxes?

Does he have any books?

He has some boxes but he doesn't have any books.

3.

Look at the girl.

Is she wearing any socks?

Is she wearing any shoes?

She is wearing some shoes but she is not wearing any socks.

some, any, no, many

1. The doll doesn't have any arms.
   It has no arms.

2. The car doesn't have any wheels.
   It has no wheels.

3. The chair doesn't have any legs.
   It has no legs.

4. She doesn't have any oranges.
   She has no oranges.

5. They don't have any tails.
   They have no tails.

6. They don't have any desks.
   They have no desks.

How many?

1.  He has a lot of books.

2. He doesn't have many books.

3. He doesn't have any books.

4. She has a lot of kittens.

5.  She doesn't have many kittens.

6. She doesn't have any kittens.

Read aloud.

ai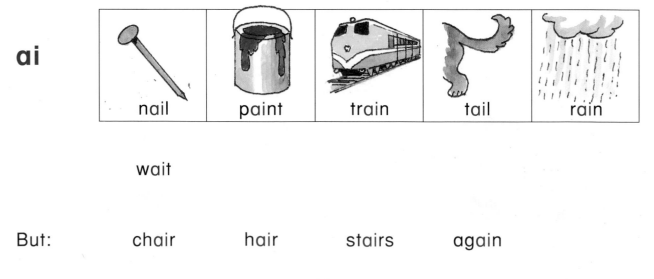

| nail | paint | train | tail | rain |

wait

But: chair   hair   stairs   again

54

A. Put in our, your, their, or its.

1. They are reading _____ books.
2. We are writing in _____ books.
3. John and Mary are sitting on _____ chairs.
4. The dog is sitting on _____ tail.
5. We are working in _____ classroom.

B. Put in some, many, or any.

1. Mrs. Lowe has _____ apples but she doesn't have _____ oranges.
2. Mrs. Bell doesn't have _____ pears but she has _____ bananas.
3. Mary is wearing _____ shoes but she is not wearing _____ socks.
4. Those cats have no tails. They don't have _____ tails.
5. "Do you want _____ apples and oranges?"
   "I want _____ apples, please, but I don't want _____ oranges.
   I have _____ oranges."

C. Choose the true answer.

1. Do you have any brothers?
   - a. No, I don't have any brothers.
   - b. Yes, I have one brother.
   - c. Yes, I have some brothers.

2. Do you have any sisters?
   - a. No, I have no sisters.
   - b. Yes, I have one sister.
   - c. Yes, I have some sisters.

1.

Is there any milk in the bottle?

Yes, there is some milk.

Is there any water in the bottle?

No, there isn't any water.

2.

Is there any ice in the glass?

Yes, there is some ice.

Is there any ink in the glass?

No, there isn't any ink.

3.

Is there any chalk in the box?

Yes, there is some chalk.

Is there any bread in the box?

No, there isn't any bread.

1. There is a lot of sand.

2. There isn't much sand.

3. There isn't any sand.

4. There is a lot of smoke.

5. There isn't much smoke.

6. There isn't any smoke.

7. There is a lot of rice.

8. There isn't much rice.

1. He has a lot of rice

   but he doesn't have much milk.

2. She has a lot of glasses

   but she doesn't have many cups.

3. He has a lot of chalk

   but he doesn't have much ink.

4. He has a lot of letters

   but he doesn't have many stamps.

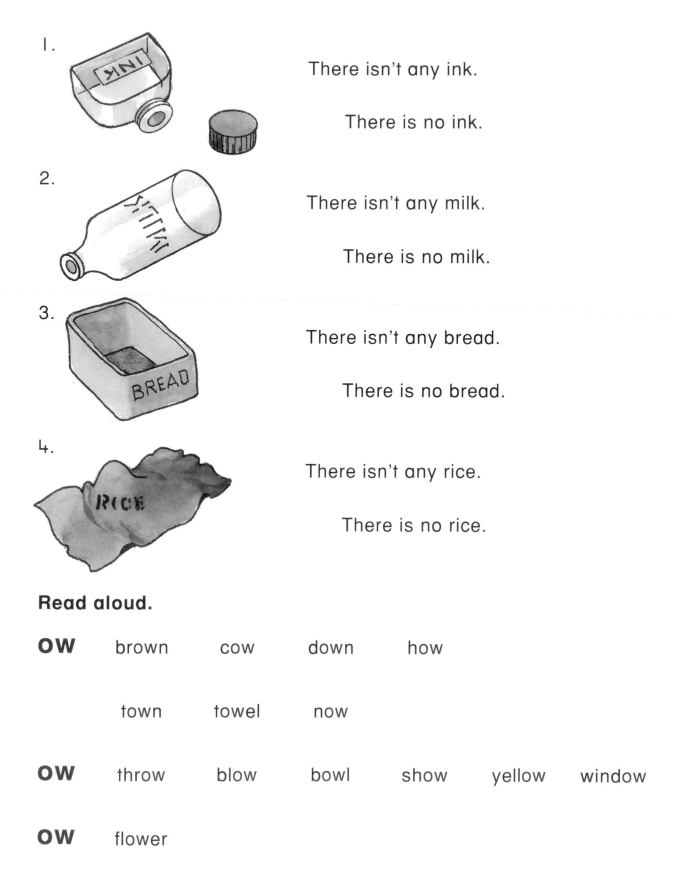

1. There isn't any ink.

   There is no ink.

2. There isn't any milk.

   There is no milk.

3. There isn't any bread.

   There is no bread.

4. There isn't any rice.

   There is no rice.

Read aloud.

OW brown   cow   down   how

      town   towel   now

OW throw   blow   bowl   show   yellow   window

OW flower

1. Are there any flowers in the picture?

   Yes, there are. There are some flowers.

2. Are there any flowers in the glass?

   No, there aren't. There aren't any flowers.

3. Are there any people on the bus?

   Yes, there are. There are some people.

4. Are there any people in the car?

   No, there aren't. There aren't any people.

5. Are there any desks in your classroom?

   Yes, there are. There are some desks.

6. Are there any cats in your classroom?

   No, there aren't. There aren't any cats.

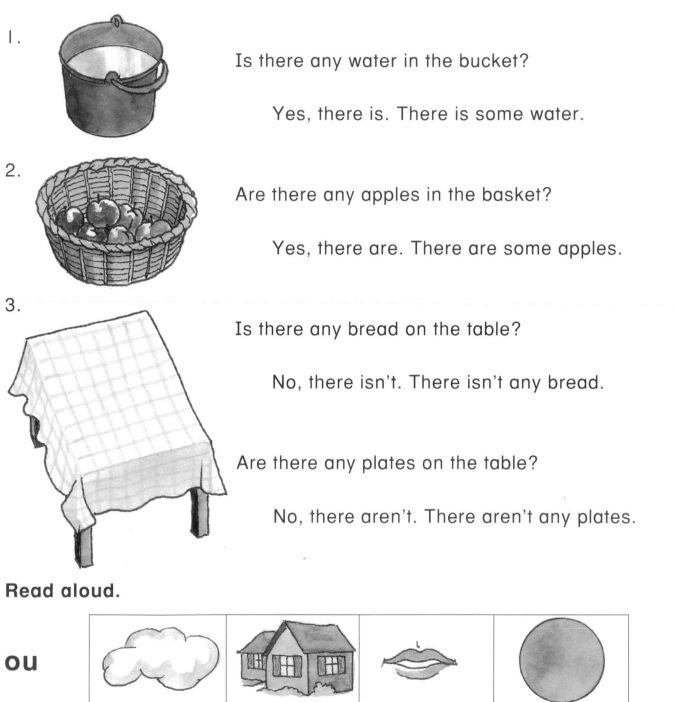

1. Is there any water in the bucket?

   Yes, there is. There is some water.

2. Are there any apples in the basket?

   Yes, there are. There are some apples.

3. Is there any bread on the table?

   No, there isn't. There isn't any bread.

   Are there any plates on the table?

   No, there aren't. There aren't any plates.

Read aloud.

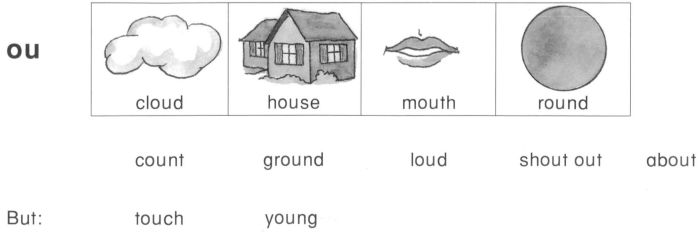

ou

| cloud | house | mouth | round |

count   ground   loud   shout out   about

But: touch   young

Are there? There aren't

1.

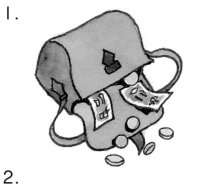

Are there any stamps in the bag?

No, there aren't any stamps but there is some money.

2.

Are there any fish in the bowl?

No, there aren't any fish but there is some water.

3.

Are there any apples on the plate?

No, there aren't any apples but there is some sugar.

4.

Are there any books on the desk?

No, there aren't any books but there is some paper.

5.

Are there any eggs in the bowl?

No, there aren't any eggs but there is some fruit.

1. Is there any water in the glass?

   No, there isn't any water but there are some pencils.

2. Is there any food on the table?

   No, there isn't any food but there are some knives and forks.

3. Is there any grass in the garden?

   No, there isn't any grass but there are some flowers.

4. Is there any water in the boat?

   No, there isn't any water but there are some men.

5. Is there any paper in the box?

   No, there isn't any paper but there are some matches.

6. Is there any bread on the table?

   No, there isn't any bread but there are some plates.

Are there? There aren't

1.

How many cookies are there on the plate?
How many cookies are there on the table?

There are a lot of cookies on the plate but there aren't many on the table.

2.

How many flowers are there in the garden?
How many flowers are there by the road?

There are a lot of flowers in the garden but there aren't many by the road.

3.

How many crackers are there in the tin?
How many crackers are there on the plate?

There are a lot of crackers in the tin but there aren't many on the plate.

4.

How many pictures are there on the wall?
How many pictures are there on the door?

There are a lot of pictures on the wall but there aren't many on the door.

Are there? There aren't

1.

How much water is there in the glass?
How much water is there in the bottle?

There is a lot of water in the glass but there isn't much in the bottle.

2.

How much food is there on the plate?
How much food is there on the table?

There is a lot of food on the plate but there isn't much on the table.

3.

How much bread is there in the basket?
How much bread is there on the plate?

There is a lot of bread in the basket but there isn't much on the plate.

4.

How much milk is there in the jug?
How much milk is there in the glass?

There is a lot of milk in the jug but there isn't much in the glass.

A. Finish these sentences. They are about your classroom.

   1. There are some desks in our classroom

   2. There aren't any . . .

   3. There is some . . .

   4. There isn't any . . .

   5. There aren't many . . .

   6. There isn't much . . .

B. Make up some sentences about your teacher's desk.

   Use these words: books, pencils, cats, pens, chalk, ink, rice.

   Example: There are some books on the teacher's desk

C. What am I?

   1. I have some legs but I don't have any arms.
     What am I?   A table.

   2. I have a mouth but I don't have any teeth.
     What am I?   A river.

   3. I have an eye but I don't have any ears.
     What am I?   A needle.

   4. I have a head but I don't have a neck.
     What am I?   A nail or a pin.

I.

It is time for school.
She is going to school.

Now she is at school.

2.

It is time for work.
He is going to work.

Now he is at work.

3.

It is time for bed.
He is going to bed.

Now he is in bed.

1.

How are they going to school?

They are going on foot.

2.

How are they going to school?

They are going to school by bus.

3.

How is he going to work?

He is going to work by car.

4.

How are they crossing the river?

They are crossing the river by boat.

5.

How are they going to the city?

They are going to the city by train.

1.

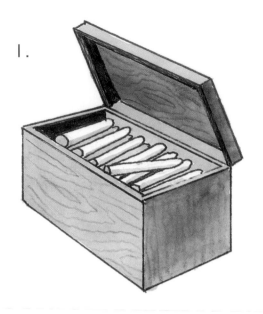

What is the box made of?

It is made of wood.

What is it full of?

It is full of chalk.

2.

What is the glass made of?

It is made of glass.

What is it full of?

It is full of milk.

3.

What is the can made of?

It is made of tin.

What is it full of?

It is full of coffee.

COFFEE

by bus, made of, etc.

A rhyme to learn.

Some people go to school by bus.

Some people go by train.

Some people go by car, 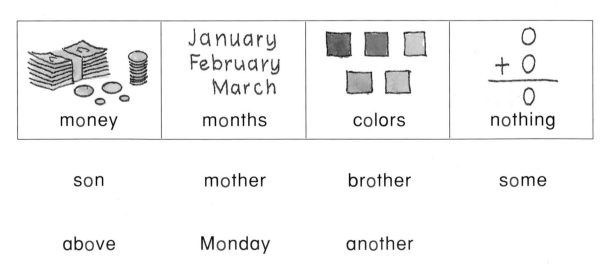 some go on foot,

but no one goes by plane.

1. What is your desk made of?
2. What is your pencil made of?
3. What is a bottle made of?
4. What is a can made of?

Read aloud.

o = u

 money	January February March months	 colors	O + O ——— O nothing
son	mother	brother	some
above	Monday	another	

70

Answer the questions.

1. Where is the girl going?

2. Where is the girl now?

3. Where is the boy going?

4. Where is the boy now?

5. What is the bottle full of?

6. What is the desk made of?

7. Can horses fly?
8. Can birds fly?
9. Can a bird read a book?
10. Can your teacher see you now?

Finish the sentences.

1. Mr. Lowe is going to work
   by _____ .

2. John is going to school on
   _____ .

3. These children are going to
   the town _____ .

4. These people are going home
   by _____ .

5. These children are going across
   the river by _____ .

6. Mr. Bell is going to
   the United States _____ .

May I?

1.

May I go outside, please?

Yes, you may.

2.

May I have an ice cream cone, please?

Yes, you may.

3.

Good morning, Miss Lee. May I carry your bag?

Good morning, Peter. Thank you. Yes, you may.

4.

May I open a window please?

Yes, John. You may.

5. Ask your teacher.

May I	open the door, close the window, have a pencil,	please?

Now ask some different things.

Read aloud.

–er

finger	driver	flower	ruler
hammer	paper	numbers	river
eraser	saucer	shoulder	letters

water	dinner	another	father
teacher	brother	sister	over

74

1. He is a doctor.

a doctor

2. She is a nurse.

a nurse

3. He is a soldier.

a soldier

4. He is a sailor.

a sailor

5. He is a fruitseller.

a fruitseller

6. He is a gardener.

a gardener

7. He is a shopkeeper.

a shopkeeper

8. She is a homemaker.

a homemaker

a teacher, a doctor, etc.

1. He is a fisherman.   a fisherman

2. He is a laborer.   a laborer

3. He is a farmer.   a farmer

4. He is a pilot.   a pilot

5. He is a firefighter.   a firefighter

6. She is a student.   a student

7. He is a baker.   a baker

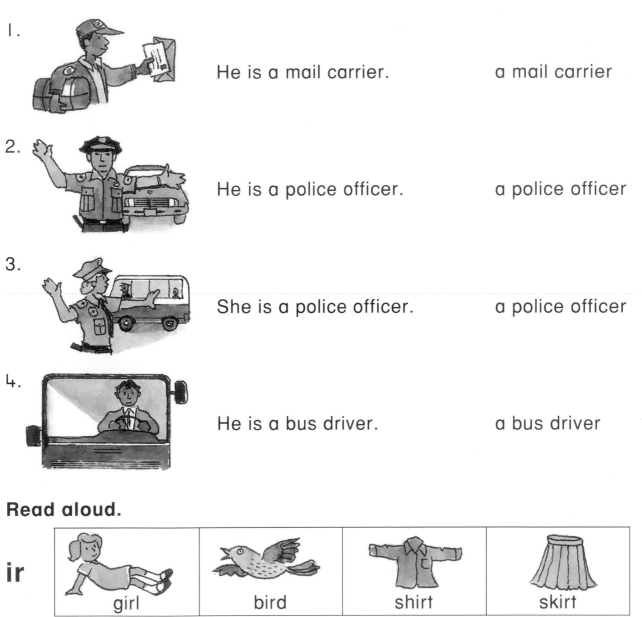

1. He is a mail carrier.   a mail carrier

2. He is a police officer.   a police officer

3. She is a police officer.   a police officer

4. He is a bus driver.   a bus driver

Read aloud.

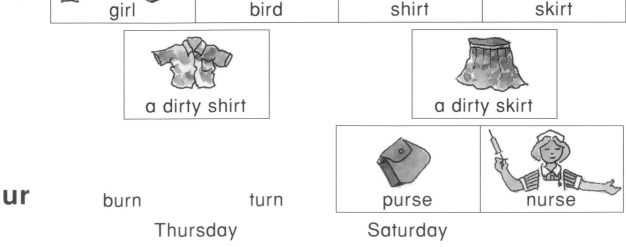

ir   girl   bird   shirt   skirt

a dirty shirt   a dirty skirt

ur   burn   turn   purse   nurse

Thursday   Saturday

Ask and answer questions like these.

Is he a bus driver?

No, he isn't.

He is a farmer.

a bus driver?

1. a teacher?

2. a farmer?

3. a mail carrier?

4. a nurse?

5. a gardener?

6. a sailor?

7. a fisherman?

8. a fruitseller?

9. a pilot?

10. a police officer?

11. a nurse?

12. a soldier?

A. Put in am, is, or are.

1. I am a doctor. I am working in a hospital.

2. I _____ a shopkeeper. I _____ working in a shop.

3. He _____ a fisherman. He _____ working on a boat.

4. She _____ a farmer. She _____ working on a farm.

5. They _____ sailors. They _____ working on a ship.

6. They _____ nurses. They _____ helping the doctor.

B. Put in has or have.

1. They are soldiers. They _____ guns.

2. He is a shopkeeper. He _____ a shop.

3. He is a pilot. He _____ a plane.

4. They are fishermen. They _____ boats.

5. He is a farmer. He _____ a farm.

C. Where can you see these?

a fisherman   a teacher   a pilot

a sailor   a shopkeeper   a nurse

Comparison of adjectives

1.

The boy is taller than the girl.

The girl is shorter than the boy.

2.

The ruler is longer than the pencil.

The pencil is shorter than the ruler.

3.

The book is thicker than the newspaper.

The newspaper is thinner than the book.

4.

The tree is bigger than the flower.

The flower is smaller than the tree.

5.

The man is stronger than the boy.

The boy is weaker than the man.

6.

The girl is younger than the woman.

The woman is older than the girl.

Comparison of adjectives

1. An airplane is faster than a car.

   A car is slower than an airplane.

2. The yellow shirt is cleaner than the white one.

   The white shirt is dirtier than the yellow one.

3. The girl is happy

   but the boy is happier.

4. The girl is hungry

   but the boy is hungrier.

5. This car is dirty

   but this one is dirtier.

6. This stone is heavy

   but this one is heavier.

Comparison of adjectives

1.

   This face is ugly

   but this one is uglier.

2.

   This picture is beautiful

   but this one is more beautiful.

3.

   This man is clever

   but this one is cleverer.

4.

   This is dangerous

   but this is more dangerous.

5.

   This boy is being careful

   but this one is being more careful.

6.

   This boy is being careless

   but this one is being more careless.

1.  This is good

    but this is better.

2. This is bad

    but this is worse.

3.
    ```
    abcde
    fghij
    ```
    This writing is good

    but this is better.
    ```
    abcde
    fghij
    ```

4.
    ```
    abcde
    fghij
    ```
    This writing is bad

    but this is worse.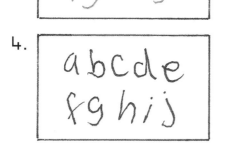

Read aloud.

or

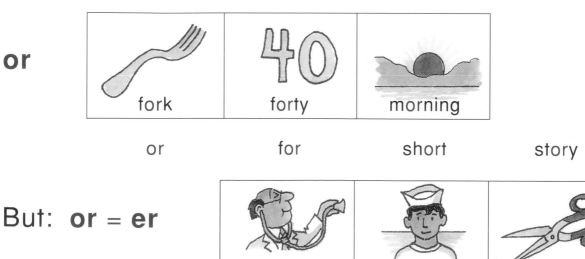

fork	forty	morning
or	for	short

story

But: or = er

doctor	sailor	scissors

Here is ... Here are ...

1. Here is a marker.

   Please draw a flower.

2. Here are some books.

   Please put them on the desk.

3. Here is an eraser.

   Please clean the board.

4.  Here is a bandage.

   Please put it on my finger.

5.  Here is some money.

   Please buy some envelopes.

6.  Here is a chain.

   Please tie up the dog.

Teacher:	Here is a pair of glasses.
	Are they your glasses, Mary?
Mary:	Yes, Miss Lee. They are my glasses.
Children:	Yes, Miss Lee. They are Mary's glasses.

Teacher:	Here is a handkerchief.
	Is it your handkerchief, John?
John:	Yes, Miss Lee. It is my handkerchief.
Children:	Yes, Miss Lee. It is his handkerchief.

Read aloud.

au   saucer   daughter   naughty   August   autumn

fall   spring   summer   winter

But: laugh

1.

May I have some thread, please?

Here it is!

2.

May I have a piece of meat, please?

Here it is!

3.

May I have a bag of flour, please?

Here it is!

4.

May I have two blankets, please?

Here they are!

5.

May I have some ripe apples, please?

Here they are!

6.

 That is $2.50, please.

Here it is!

Where is Mary?	There she is!
Where is Peter?	There he is!
Where is Ann?	There she is!
Where are John and Betty?	There they are!

Read aloud.

tr	train	tree	truck
dr	dress	drum	drawer	drinking	drive dry drawing
gr	grass	green	gray	grandfather grandson grandmother granddaughter
br	bread	brown	brush	breakfast brother bring

87

1.

Is there anything under the table?
Yes, there is.
There is something under the table.
It is a cat.

2.

Is there anything under the desk?
No, there isn't.
There isn't anything under the desk.
There is nothing under the desk.

3.

Is there anything on the chair?
Yes, there is.
There is something on the chair.
It is a basket.

4.

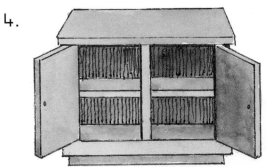

Is there anything in the cupboard?
No, there isn't.
There isn't anything in the cupboard.
There is nothing in the cupboard.

someone, anyone, no one

1. Is there anyone on the bus?
   Yes, there is.
   There is someone on the bus.

2. Is there anyone in the car?
   No, there isn't.
   There isn't anyone in the car.
   There is no one in the car.

3. Is there anyone on the sidewalk?
   Yes, there is.
   There is someone on the sidewalk.

4. Is there anyone in the truck?
   No, there isn't.
   There isn't anyone in the truck.
   There is no one in the truck.

**Ask questions about the pictures. Use anything or anyone.
Then answer the questions.**

1.	2.	3.	4.
anyone	anything	anyone	anything

5.	6.	7.	8.
anything	anything	anyone	anyone

1. Is there anyone on the train?
   No, there isn't.
   There isn't anyone on the train.
   There is no one on the train.

Read aloud.

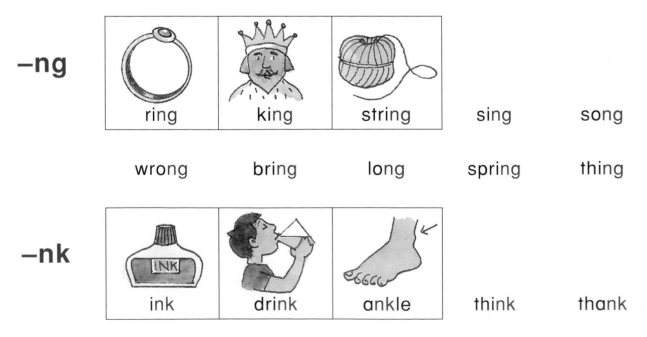

–ng

ring   king   string   sing   song

wrong   bring   long   spring   thing

–nk

ink   drink   ankle   think   thank

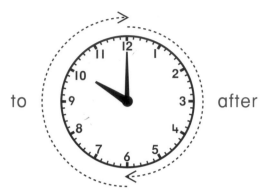

to   after

What time is it?
It is ten o'clock.

Look at the clock.
There are two hands,
a big one and a small one.
There are twelve hours.
There are sixty minutes.

It is twelve o'clock.

It is five after twelve.

It is ten after twelve.

It is a quarter after twelve.

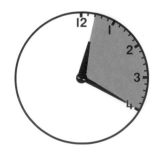

It is twenty after twelve.

It is twenty-five after twelve.

What time is it?

It is twelve-thirty.

It is twenty-five to one.

It is twenty to one.

It is a quarter to one.

It is ten to one.

It is five to one.

Read aloud.

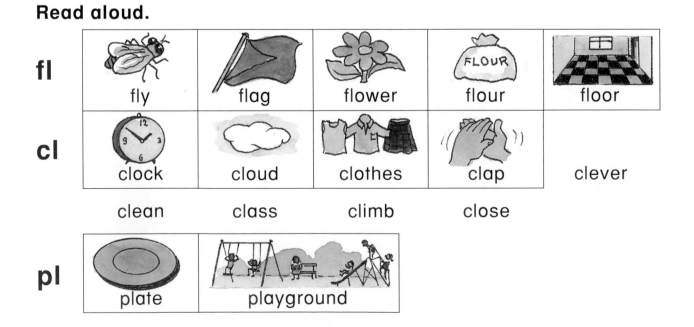

fl	fly	flag	flower	flour	floor
cl	clock	cloud	clothes	clap	clever

clean   class   climb   close

pl	plate	playground

add +; subtract −; multiply ×; divide ÷.

1. Start with one. Add two. Subtract three.

   Is there anything left?

2. Start with three. Multiply by two. Subtract five.

   Is there anything left?

3. Start with four. Add six. Divide by two. Subtract five.

   Is there anything left?

Review

Look at your classroom and answer the questions.

1. Is there anyone in front of you?
2. Is there anyone behind you?
3. Is there anyone on your left?
4. Is there anyone on your right?
5. Is there anything on the blackboard?
6. Is there anything on the wall?
7. Is there anything on the desk?
8. Is there anything on the floor?
9. Is there anyone outside the classroom?
10. Is there anything in your right hand?
11. Is there anything in your left hand?
12. Is there anything in your pocket?

Ask and answer questions about the pictures.

1. What time is it?

It is eight o'clock.

It is time for breakfast.

Read aloud.

–le	bottle	circle	table	needle	whistle
	bicycle	handle	ankle	apple	little apple

1.

Where is the book?
The book is on the desk.
Put it on the chair.

2.

The book was on the desk.
Now it is on the chair.
Put it on the table.

3.

The book was on the chair.
Now it is on the table.

4.

Where are the boys?
They are in the tree.

5.

Where were the boys?
They were in the tree.
Where are the boys now?
They are on the roof.

6.

Where were the boys?
They were on the roof.
Where are they now?
They are in the car.

A. Answer Yes, I was or No, I was not.

    1. Were you in bed at five o'clock this morning?

    2. Were you in bed at eight o'clock this morning?

    3. Were you in school at seven o'clock this morning?

    4. Were you in school at nine o'clock this morning?

B. Answer Yes, they were or No, they were not.

    1. Were your friends in school at nine o'clock this morning?

    2. Were your friends in school at six o'clock this morning?

    3. Were your friends in school last Thursday?

    4. Were your friends in school last Sunday?

C. Answer Yes, it was or No, it was not.

    1. Was it Saturday yesterday?

    2. Was it a holiday yesterday?

    3. Was it a school day yesterday?

    4. Was it cold yesterday?

Finish the sentences.

1. Today is _____ day.

2. Yesterday was _____ .

3. The day before yesterday _____ _____ .

4. Three days ago it was _____ .

5. Four days ago _____ _____ _____ .

6. This year is 19 __ __ .

7. Last year was 19 __ __ .

8. The year before last _____ 19 __ __ .

9. Ten years ago it _____ 19 __ __ .

10. Last _____ day _____ a holiday.

Read aloud.

sw

| swim | sweep |

sm   smile   small   smell   smoke

sp   speak   spoon   sl   slow   sleep

su

| sun | subtract | summer   Sunday

But: sugar   Be careful with: school   scissors

1.

I had three apples
    but I was hungry.
Now I have two.

John

2.

Mary had five eggs
    but she was careless.
Now she has four.

Mary

3.

Tom had ten cookies
    but he was hungry.
Now he has one.

Tom

4.

Ann had three flowers
    but she was careless.
Now she has two.

Ann

5.

The men had two boats
    but there was a hole in one.
Now they have one.

The men

had

Look at page 98.

Did John have three apples?
Yes, he did. He had three apples.

Did Mary have six eggs?
No, she did not. She had five eggs.

Did Tom have ten cookies?
Yes, he did. He had ten cookies.

Did Ann have four flowers?
No, she did not. She had three flowers.

Did the men have two boats?
Yes, they did. They had two boats.

Answer these questions.

1. How many apples did John have?
2. How many eggs did Mary have?
3. How many cookies did Tom have?
4. How many flowers did Ann have?
5. How many boats did the men have?

Give short answers.

1. Were you in school yesterday?

   Yes, I was or No, I was not.

2. Did you have any money in your pocket yesterday?

   Yes, I did or No, I did not.

3. Did the mail carrier have a letter for you this morning?

4. Were your friends in school yesterday?

5. Did your teacher have white shoes yesterday?

6. Was your teacher in the classroom yesterday?

7. Did you have a cat in your desk yesterday?

8. Did your teacher have a piece of chalk yesterday?

Read aloud.

–rt	shirt	short	skirt	start
–rd	bird	hard	word	cupboard
–rn	turn	learn	**–rm**	arm
–rk	mark	work	**–rl**	girl

	first	second	third	fourth	fifth
1.	short	very short	tall	very tall	not very
2.	fat	very fat	thin	very thin	not very
3.	small	very small	big	very big	not very
4.	$\frac{80}{100}$ good	$\frac{100}{100}$ very good	$\frac{30}{100}$ bad	$\frac{0}{100}$ very bad	$\frac{60}{100}$ not very

1. The first boy is short.

   The second boy is very short.

   The third boy is tall.

   The fourth boy is very tall.

   The fifth is not very short and not very tall.

Now make sentences about the women in No. 2, the cars in No. 3, and the marks in No. 4.

A. Answer the questions.

    1. Do you like school?   Yes, I like it very much.
    2. Do you like cookies?   Yes, I like them very much.
    3. Do you like snakes?   No, I don't like them.
    4. Do you like bananas?
    5. Do you like English?
    6. Do you like math?
    7. Do you like the radio?
    8. Do you like your teacher?
    9. Do you like dogs?
  10. Do you like cats?

B. Make five sentences beginning: I like . . .
    Make five sentences beginning: I don't like . . .

C. Make sentences about these pictures.

wet   hot   beautiful   big

Read aloud.

—11   ball   bell   doll   all   tall

           fall   small   smell   kill

D. Make sentences like these about the pictures below.

      1. The balloon is very small.

      2. The man is very old.

You may use any of these words. You may use some more than once.

small	old	long	brave	big	fast
greedy	clean	heavy	cold	short	happy
ugly	tall	wet	strong		

1. balloon	2. man	3. skirt	4. firefighter	5. collar
6. car	7. boy	8. glass	9. bag	10. ice
11. nurse	12. sailor	13. face	14. soldier	15. man
16. laborer	17. woman	18. hammer	19. hole	20. jug
21. kitten	22. pants	23. package	24. plane	25. girl

Review

A. Ask and answer questions like these.

What is this?
  It is a piece of chalk.

What is this?
  It is a bowl of soup.

1.

2.

3.

4.

5.

6.

7.

8.

9.

10.

11.

12.

B. Answer the questions.

1. Can you sing?   Yes, I can.   No, I cannot.
2. Can you swim?
3. Can you cook?
4. Can you see an airplane?
5. Can you hear an airplane?

C. How many true sentences can you make? Use different words in the boxes.

I like **?** but my

friend
brother
sister
mother
father

likes **?**

D. What are they saying? The first two are done for you.

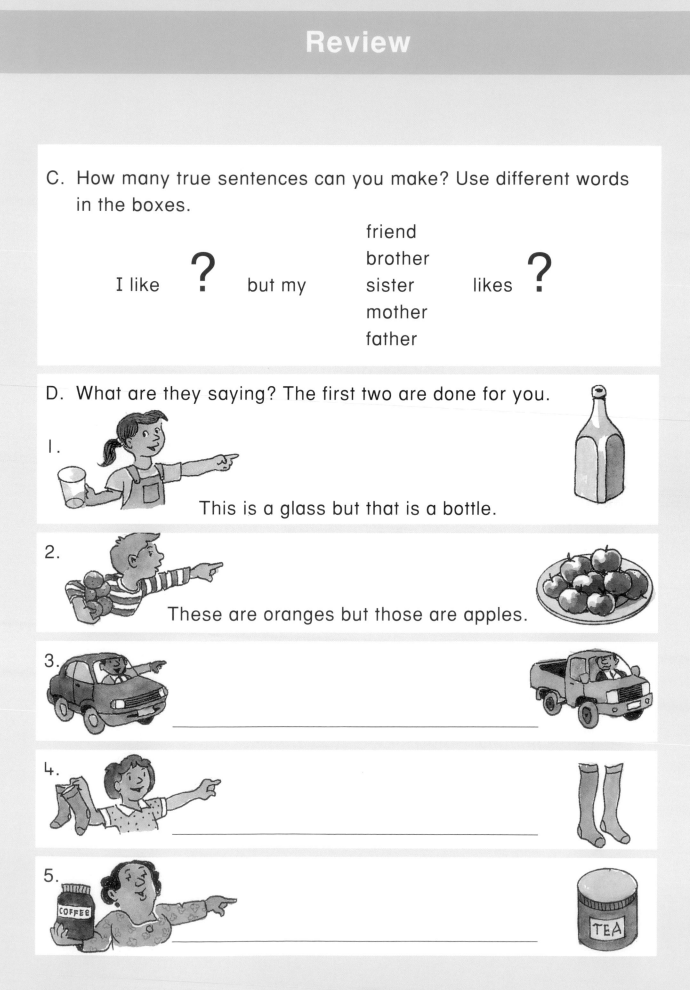

1. This is a glass but that is a bottle.

2. These are oranges but those are apples.

3. _____

4. _____

5. _____

E. Ask and answer questions like these.

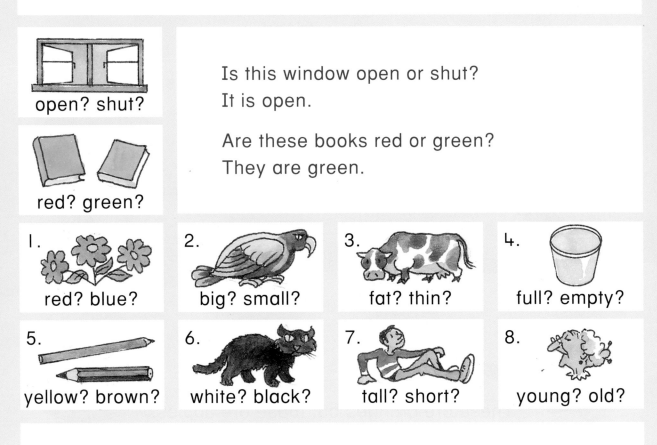

open? shut?

red? green?

Is this window open or shut?
It is open.

Are these books red or green?
They are green.

1. red? blue?

2. big? small?

3. fat? thin?

4. full? empty?

5. yellow? brown?

6. white? black?

7. tall? short?

8. young? old?

F. Put in the right words.

1. That is Tom. Can you see him?

2. There is Mary. Can you see _____ ?

3. There are a lot of people in the room. I can hear _____ .

4. The teacher is saying something but I cannot hear _____ .

5. We are behind the trees. No one can see _____ .

6. Don't close the window. Please open _____ .

7. I cannot see my dog. Can you see _____ ?

8. There is John. The teacher is talking to _____ ?

Review

G. Finish the sentences about the pictures.

John   Peter   Mary   Ann

 1. John has a red hat and his shoes are red, too.
 2. John has a blue shirt and . . .
 3. Peter has a green hat and . . .
 4. Peter has white socks and . . .
 5. Mary has a blue skirt and her . . .
 6. Mary has a white hat and . . .
 7. Ann has a red skirt and . . .
 8. Ann has yellow socks and . . .
 9. John has a boat and Peter has one, too.
10. Peter has an airplane and . . .
11. Mary has a doll and . . .
12. Ann has a kitten . . .

H. Put in my, your, its, our, or their.
 1. Look at the children. Can you see _____ hats?
 2. That cat is sitting on _____ tail.
 3. We work in this classroom. It is _____ classroom.
 4. "This is not my book. Is it your book?" "Yes, it is.

        It is _____ book."

I. Ask and answer questions about the pictures.

1. grass in the garden? (flowers)

2. cups on the table? (bread)

3. bread in the cupboard? (bottles)

4. animals in the picture? (trees)

5. rice on the plate? (crackers)

6. cookies on the table? (milk)

7. paper on the desk? (pencils)

8. eggs in the bowl? (rice)

1. Is there any grass in the garden?
   No, there isn't any grass in the garden but there are some flowers.
2. Are there any cups on the table?
   No, there aren't any cups on the table but there is some bread.

J. Ask and answer questions like these about the pictures on page 108.

    1. Are there many flowers in the garden?
        Yes, there are. There are a lot of flowers in the garden.
    2. Is there much bread on the table?
        No, there isn't. There isn't much bread on the table.
    3. Are there many bottles in the cupboard?
        No, there aren't. There aren't many bottles in the cupboard.

K. Read. Then answer the questions.

1.

    What is John?
        He is a student.
    What time is it?
        It is eight o'clock.
        It is time for school.
    Where is John going?
        He is going to school.

2.

    What is Mr. Lee?

    What time is it?

    Where is Mr. Lee going?

L. Give answers like these.

   1. Is a pencil longer than a ruler? No, a pencil is shorter than a ruler.

   2. Is a man shorter than a boy?   No, a man is taller than a boy.

   3. Is a newspaper thicker than a book?

   4. Is a man weaker than a boy?

   5. Is a car faster than an airplane?

   6. Is a girl taller than a woman?

   7. Is a tree smaller than a flower?

M. Ask and answer questions like these.

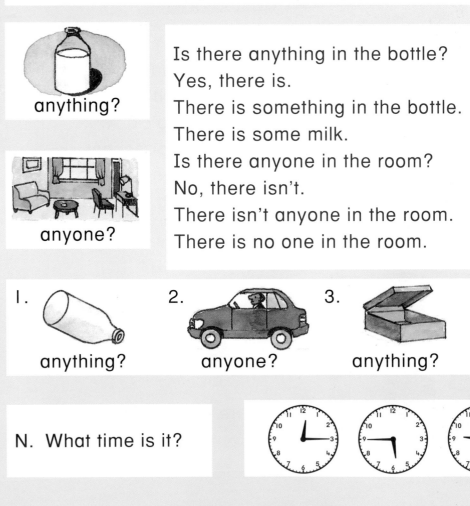

anything?

Is there anything in the bottle?
Yes, there is.
There is something in the bottle.
There is some milk.
Is there anyone in the room?
No, there isn't.
There isn't anyone in the room.
There is no one in the room.

anyone?

1. anything?   2. anyone?   3. anything?   4. anyone?

N. What time is it?

O. Add was, is, had, or has.

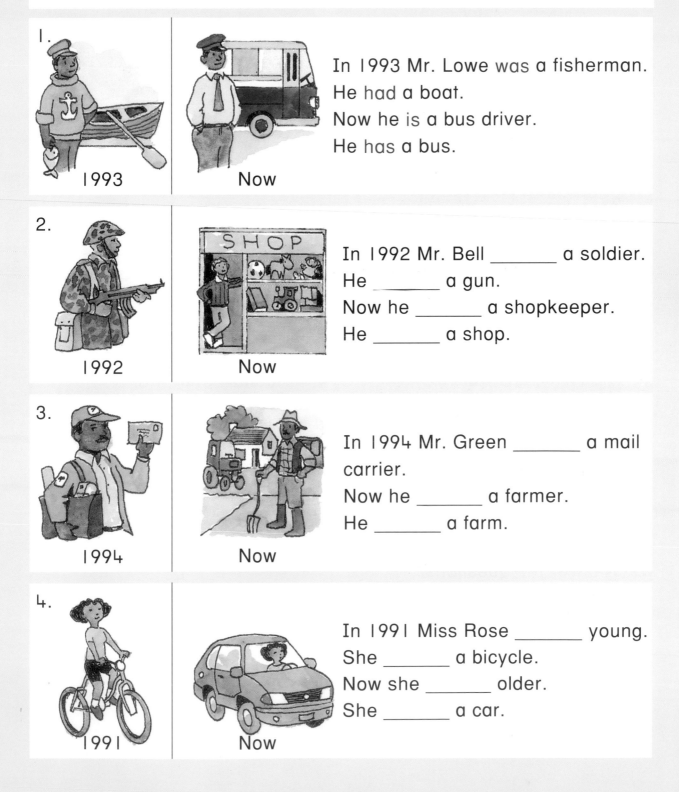

1.

1993   Now

In 1993 Mr. Lowe was a fisherman.
He had a boat.
Now he is a bus driver.
He has a bus.

2.

1992   Now

In 1992 Mr. Bell _____ a soldier.
He _____ a gun.
Now he _____ a shopkeeper.
He _____ a shop.

3.

1994   Now

In 1994 Mr. Green _____ a mail
carrier.
Now he _____ a farmer.
He _____ a farm.

4.

1991   Now

In 1991 Miss Rose _____ young.
She _____ a bicycle.
Now she _____ older.
She _____ a car.

P. Make sentences about the pictures like these.

Peter – tall

1994   Now

In 1994 Peter was tall.

Now he is very tall.

1. Miss Lowe – thin

1992   Now

2. Mrs. Rose – fat

1993   Now

3. This car – old

1980   Now

4. John's shirt – dirty

Yesterday   Now

Q. Answer the questions.

  1. Do you like bananas?   Yes, I like bananas very much.

                     or   No, I don't like bananas very much.

  2. Do you like chocolate?

  3. Do you like school?

  4. Do you like football?

  5. Do you like picnics?

Word List

A	above	70			
	across	30			
	add	93			
	after	91			
	ago	97			
	always	32			
	ankle	25			
	any	50			
	anyone	89			
	anything	88			
	asleep	38			
	August	85			
	autumn	85			

B
baker 76
bandage 84
beautiful 82
before 97
better 83
blanket 86
brave 103
break 31
bucket 37
burn 77
but 18
buy 84
by 68

C
can 13
cannot 13
careful 31

careless 31
catch 35
centimeter 37
chain 84
circle 20
clever 82
climbing 7
collar 20
cone 73
cracker 64
cross 68

D
dance 38
dangerous 30
date 32
different 42
divide 93
doctor 20
dollars 86
drum 20
dry 27

E
empty 24
envelope 84

F
fall 85
farm 79
fast 81
fifth 101
fight 30
firefighter 76

first 101
fisherman 76
flag 42
flour 86
fly 19
food 63
for 67
fork 63
fourth 101
fruit 62
fruitseller 75
full 24
full of 69

G
garden 63
gardener 75
gate 40
glass 69
glasses 85
granddaughter 87
grandfather 87
grandmother 87
grandson 87
gray 87
ground 61
gun 79

H
hammer 20
handle 94
hear 13
heavy 81

Word List

	hole	98	meat	86	quiet	31
	homemaker	75	milk	11		
	horse	21	minute	91	**R** rice	57
	hospital	79	more	82	ring	90
	hour	91	much	57	ripe	86
	hungry	81	multiply	93	round	21
I	ink	11	**N** nail	20	**S** sailor	75
	inside	45	naughty	30	same	42
			needle	20	sand	57
J	jug	65	new	24	Saturday	77
			no one	70	scissors	83
K	king	20	nurse	75	second	101
	kitten	21			see	13
	kneel	38	**O** or	25	sew	38
	knife	63	out	29	shopkeeper	75
			outside	73	shoulder	74
L	laborer	76			sidewalk	30
	last	97	**P** package	37	skirt	40
	late	31	paper	11	slow	81
	left	93	path	30	smoke	57
	letter	40	people	60	sock	23
	like	15	piece	11	soldier	75
	little	44	pilot	76	someone	89
	lot	53	plane	70	something	88
			purse	77	sound	31
M	made of	69	put	84	soup	11
	many	54			spring	85
	marker	18	**Q** quarter	91	square	20
	math	102	queen	20	stamp	40
	may	73	quick	31	start	93

Word List

	string	11
	strong	21
	subtract	93
	summer	85
T	tea	12
	teach	34
	than	80
	Thank you	16
	that	22
	thing	90
	think	90
	third	101
	those	23
	thread	86
	tie (noun)	20
	tie (verb)	84
	tin	64
	today	97
	too	37
	truck	20
	turn	77
U	ugly	82
	use	32
W	want	52
	water	11
	weak	21
	wet	27

	whistle	37
	winter	85
	wood	11
	work	68
	worse	83
Y	year	21
	yesterday	96